**NATIONAL
GEOGRAPHIC**

D0503680

Using Rocks

Jacob Fink

Contents

People dig rocks out of the earth.
There are many types of rocks.
People use rocks in different ways.

Marble

Marble is a smooth rock.
Marble can be many different colors.
How do people use marble?

People cut blocks of marble out of the ground.

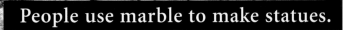

People use marble to make statues.

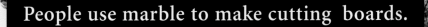

People use marble to make cutting boards.

Slate

Slate is a flaky rock.
Slate can be many different colors.
How do people use slate?

People dig slate out of the earth.

People use slate to make walls.

People use slate to make roofs.

Granite

Granite is a very hard rock.
Granite is made of large different-colored grains.
How do people use granite?

People dig granite out of the earth.

People use granite to make columns.

People use granite to make buildings.

Sandstone

Sandstone is a grainy rock.
Sandstone is made of grains of sand.
How do people use sandstone?

People dig sandstone out of the earth.

People use sandstone to make bowls.

People use sandstone to make plant holders.

Index